LIGHTNING
BOLT
BOOKS™

# The Grand Canyon

Jeffrey Zuehlke

Lerner Publications Company
Minneapolis

For Gus,
future long-distance hiker
—J.Z.

Lerner Publications Company
A division of Lerner Publishing Group, Inc.
241 First Avenue North
Minneapolis, MN 55401 U.S.A.

Website address: www.lernerbooks.com

Library of Congress Cataloging-in-Publication Data

Zuehlke, Jeffrey, 1968–
  The Grand Canyon / by Jeffrey Zuehlke.
    p.   cm. — (Lightning Bolt Books ™ — Famous places)
  Includes index.
  ISBN 978-0-7613-4261-8 (lib. bdg. : alk. paper)
  1. Grand Canyon (Ariz.)—Juvenile literature.  2. Grand Canyon National Park (Ariz.)—Juvenile
literature.  I. Title.
  F788.Z84 2010
  979.132—dc22                                        2009016514

Manufactured in the United States of America
1 — BP — 12/15/09

# Contents

Welcome to the Grand Canyon — page 4

What Made the Grand Canyon? — page 10

Visiting the Grand Canyon — page 18

Map — page 28

Fun Facts — page 29

Glossary — page 30

Further Reading — page 31

Index — page 32

# Welcome to the Grand Canyon

Have you ever seen this place before?
It is the Grand Canyon.

The word *grand* means
"huge, beautiful, and amazing."
The Grand Canyon is
all of these things.

The canyon's rocky walls are tall and colorful. The canyon is 1 mile (1.6 kilometers) deep in some places.

The Grand Canyon is 277 miles (446 km) long. Some parts are 10 miles (16 km) wide.

Does that sound grand to you?

This picture of the Grand Canyon was taken from an airplane.

# The Grand Canyon is in northern Arizona. It cuts through dry desert.

Hot, dry desert surrounds the Grand Canyon.

Millions of people visit the canyon each year. They come to hike and camp. They come to see the beautiful walls. The Grand Canyon is an amazing place to visit.

People hike on a trail in the Grand Canyon.

# What Made the Grand Canyon?

Did you know that the Grand Canyon is millions of years old?

But what made the canyon? Would you believe it was the Colorado River?

The Colorado River cuts through the middle of the Grand Canyon.

The river's rushing water has slowly carved out the canyon. The water carries rock away. This is called erosion.

River waters have slowly eroded the Grand Canyon's walls.

The water acts very slowly. How slowly? It has taken the Colorado River six million years to carve out the Grand Canyon!

Can you see the colored stripes on the canyon's walls? Each stripe is a layer of rock. Each layer is a different kind of rock.

Bands of rock give the Grand Canyon its colorful look.

The newest rock is at the top of the canyon. This white-colored rock is called Kaibab limestone. This rock is about 300 feet (91 meters) thick.

The Grand Canyon's top layers are made of white Kaibab limestone.

The oldest rock is at the bottom of the canyon. This dark, hard rock is called the Vishnu schist. It is about two billion years old.

Low layers of the canyon are older than layers near the top.

The canyon has many more
layers.  One layer is called
Redwall limestone.  This rock
is more than 300 million
years old.

Red limestone walls
glow during a sunrise.

17

# Visiting the Grand Canyon

People come from all around the world to visit the Grand Canyon.

The Grand Canyon is a huge place. It would take years to see every part of it. But you can see and do a lot in just a few days.

A hiker walks along a trail in the Grand Canyon.

The Grand Canyon is a U.S. national park. The U.S. government owns and protects this land.

Grand Canyon National Park is one of the most popular national parks in the United States.

GRAND CANYON NATIONAL PARK

U.S. park rangers work here. They help visitors find their way around. They help keep the park clean and safe. Rangers also teach people all about the canyon.

A ranger at the Grand Canyon looks through a pair of binoculars.

Grand Canyon National Park has three different parts. Each part is very different.

The northern part of the park is called the North Rim. The word *rim* means "outer edge." The North Rim is the coldest part of the park.

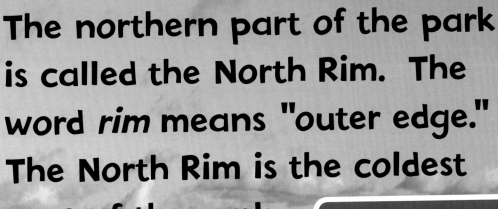

This is a view from the North Rim of the Grand Canyon.

Most people visit the South Rim.  This is the southern part of the park.  People come here to hike, camp, and explore.

Visitors to the South Rim look out over the canyon.

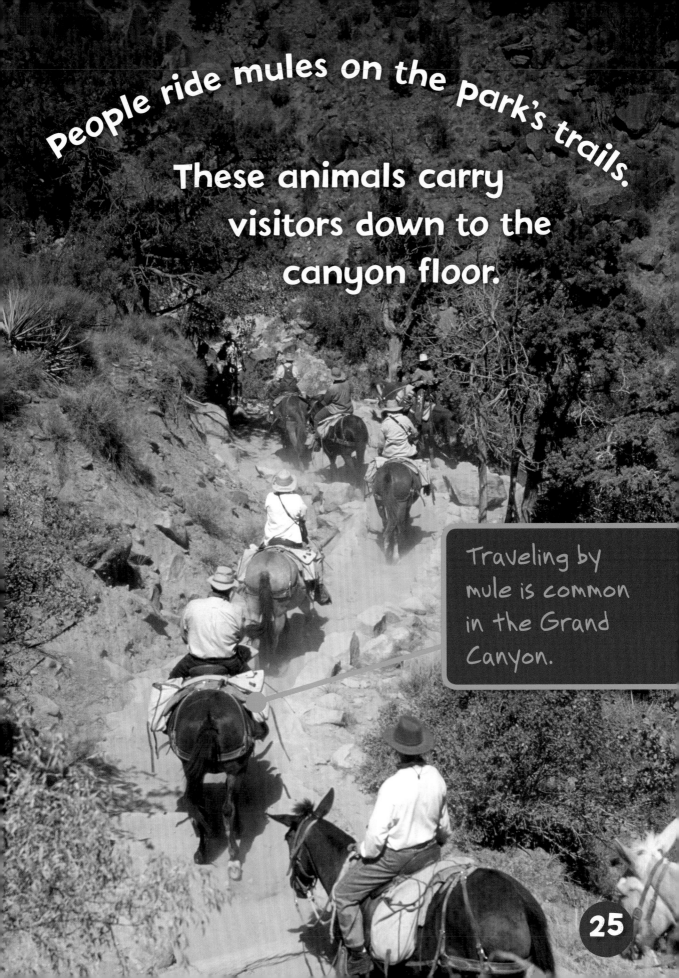

People ride mules on the park's trails. These animals carry visitors down to the canyon floor.

Traveling by mule is common in the Grand Canyon.

The canyon floor is called the Inner Canyon. This is the place to see the Colorado River up close. The Inner Canyon has many trails and streams to explore.

Elves Chasm is in the Inner Canyon. It has a pretty waterfall.

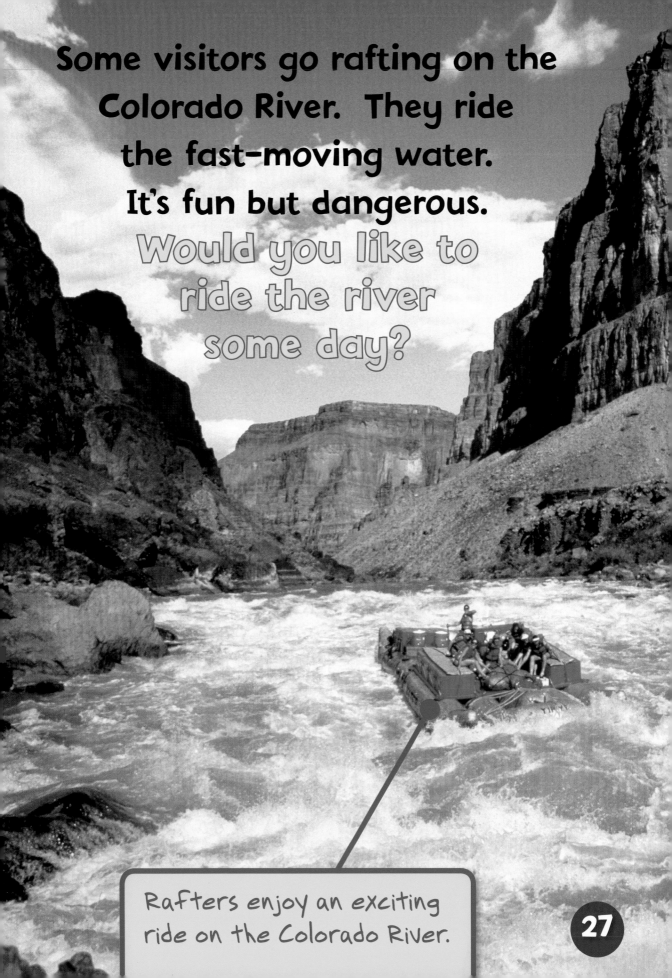

Some visitors go rafting on the Colorado River. They ride the fast-moving water. It's fun but dangerous. Would you like to ride the river some day?

Rafters enjoy an exciting ride on the Colorado River.

# The Grand Canyon Area

COLORADO

UTAH

NEVADA

ROCKY

Colorado
River

MOUNTAINS

Lake
Mead

**Grand
Canyon**

Colorado
River

ARIZONA

CALIFORNIA

NEW MEXICO

N

Arizona

**UNITED
STATES**

Miles

| 0 | 20 | 40 | 60 | 80 |
|---|----|----|----|----|
| 0 | 40 | 80 | 120 | |

Kilometers

MEXICO

# Fun Facts

- Arizona's nickname is the Grand Canyon State.

- About five million people visit the Grand Canyon each year.

- The U.S. government made the Grand Canyon a national park in 1919.

- John Wesley Powell was the first American to explore the entire Grand Canyon. In 1869, he and his team of explorers made maps of the area.

- It takes between two and three weeks to ride a raft from one end of the Grand Canyon to the other.

# Glossary

**canyon:** a deep, narrow river valley with steep sides

**desert:** a dry, sandy area

**erosion:** the process in which moving water or wind carries away land over time

**mule:** an animal that is part horse and part donkey. People ride mules on the Grand Canyon National Park's trails.

**national park:** an area that is owned, protected, and managed by the government

**park ranger:** a person who works to protect national parks and help visitors

**rafting:** riding down a river on a flat-bottomed boat called a raft

**rim:** outer edge

# Further Reading

*Grand Canyon National Park (U.S. National Park Service)*
http://www.nps.gov/grca/index.htm

*National Geographic Kids Brainteaser: Grand Canyon*
http://kids.nationalgeographic.com/Games/PuzzlesQuizzes/Brainteasergrandcanyon

Petersen, David. *Grand Canyon National Park*. New York: Children's Press, 2001.

Riley, Joelle. *Erosion*. Minneapolis: Lerner Publications Company, 2007.

Trumbauer, Lisa. *Grand Canyon*. New York: Children's Press, 2005.

Zuehlke, Jeffrey. *The Hoover Dam*. Minneapolis: Lerner Publications Company, 2010.

# Index

Arizona, 8, 29

Colorado River, 11, 13, 26–27

desert, 8

Elves Chasm, 26
erosion, 12

Grand Canyon National Park, 20, 22

Inner Canyon, 26

Kaibab limestone, 15

mules, 25

North Rim, 23

park rangers, 21
Powell, John Wesley, 29

Redwall limestone, 17

South Rim, 24

Vishnu schist, 16

# Photo Acknowledgments

The images in this book are used with the permission of: © Carmel Studios/SuperStock, pp. 4–5; © Flirt/SuperStock, pp. 6, 14; © Rich Reid/National Geographic/Getty Images, p. 7; © Ken Samuelsen/Photodisc/Getty Images, p. 8; © John Burcham/National Geographic/Getty Images, p. 9; © David Muench/Stone/Getty Images, pp. 10–11; © age fotostock/SuperStock, pp. 12, 18, 22–23, 24, 26, 30; Mike Quinn, National Park Service, p. 13; © Hemis.fr/SuperStock, pp. 15, 16–17, 21; © Prisma/SuperStock, p. 19; © Laura Ciapponi/Photonica/Getty Images, p. 20; © Demetrio Carrasco/Dorling Kindersley/Getty Images, p. 25; © John Beatty/Stone/Getty Images, p. 27; © Laura Westlund/Independent Picture Service, p. 28; © Ralph Lee Hopkins/National Geographic/Getty Images, p. 31.

Front Cover: © Prisma/SuperStock